DIRK DEVOS · MANON DE WIT · ROBERT LUBBERDING

LEADING FROM BEHIND

TURN ANXIETY INTO COURAGE

Published by
LID Publishing Limited
The Record Hall, Studio 204,
16-16a Baldwins Gardens,
London EC1N 7RJ, UK

524 Broadway, 11th Floor, Suite 08-120,
New York, NY 10012, US

info@lidpublishing.com
www.lidpublishing.com

A member of:

www.businesspublishersroundtable.com

© Dirk Devos, Manon De Wit and Robert Lubberding, 2018
© LID Publishing Limited, 2018

Printed in Latvia by Jelgavas Tipogrāfij
ISBN: 978-1-911498-90-2 (paperback)
ISBN: 978-1-911498-95-7 (hardback)

Cover and page design: Caroline Li

DIRK DEVOS · MANON DE WIT · ROBERT LUBBERDING

LEADING FROM BEHIND

TURN ANXIETY INTO COURAGE

LONDON NEW YORK SHANGHAI
MADRID BARCELONA BOGOTA
MEXICO CITY MONTERREY BUENOS AIRES

My deepest gratitude goes to those who are always there
and have accepted my focused intensity as who I am:
Nicole, Annabel, Valesca, Maxime, Ferre and Stijn.
Dirk

To my dad, mom and Wim.
Thank you for your unconditional love.
Manon

Janine,
you are the love of my life.
Thank you for accepting me for who I truly am,
with all my sunny and shady sides.
Robert

From now on,
the most effective leaders
will lead from behind,
not from the front.

He stays behind the flock,
letting the most nimble go ahead,
whereupon the others follow,
not realizing that all along they
are directed from behind.

Nelson Mandela

CONTENTS

FOREWORD
BY DR MARSHALL GOLDSMITH

Leadership is about helping others achieve their best. This applies to individuals as much as it does to teams. Leadership is simple, but not easy.

Dirk, Manon and Robert have masterfully applied the Marshall Goldsmith Stakeholder Centered Coaching methodology in their leadership and coaching practice. Now we can all learn from their experience in their book *Leading from Behind*.

In this book they introduce nine practices that help leaders achieve positive, lasting change in their behaviour. By using a cycle of feedback and feedforward on how to improve key behaviours, leaders are enabled to identify and focus on the areas that will yield the most impact.

These nine practices make leaders more conscious about the active choice we all have between a trigger and our behaviour. By using those triggers to enhance behavioural effectiveness, leaders can increase their focus on what is important instead of being distracted and wasting energy in the change process.

The concepts laid out in *Leading from Behind* fit perfectly with the Stakeholder Centered Coaching model. They provide the giver and the receiver of feedback with additional context to maximize the relevance and impact of that information. The end result is leaders living out their values and purpose with courage. Using these concepts will enrich each leaders' journey towards transformational leadership.

As leaders we know that what got us here won't get us there. If we want to get the best out of others (and out of ourselves), *Leading from Behind* is an excellent place to start.

Let the journey begin.

Life is good,
Marshall Goldsmith

Marshall Goldsmith Ph.D., bestselling author of *Triggers*

Dr. Marshall Goldsmith has been recognized by the American Management Association as one of 50 great thinkers and business leaders who have impacted the field of management over the past 80 years – and by *Business Week* as one of the most influential practitioners in the history of leadership development. Marshall was recognized as the #1 Leadership Thinker in the World and one of the top 5 Most Influential Business Thinkers in the World, as well as the #1 Executive Coach at the 2015 biennial Thinkers50 ceremony in London.

A GENUINE PEOPLE-CENTRIC APPROACH

In our professional lives, there is one question that has puzzled us: How do we get the best from everyone, everywhere, anytime?

Many people told us that we should write a book about our special way of getting the best from everyone, everywhere, anytime.

Yet we did not feel that what we had to say was unique enough because, in our view, most of what we had to share we had learned from our masters.

After many years, we can now see that our unique contribution may be the simple practice model we have developed from the essential teachings and insights of those thought leaders: the 'Leading from Behind' approach. This model emerged through our experiences as transformational leadership consultants and has since proved its effectiveness, again and again.

We are excited to share our findings in this book; we believe they have the potential to become the next perspective on transformational leadership. Our clients say these practices are impactful, transformative, unique in their kind and combination, simple though not simplistic, robust, and designed for exponential scaling.

We have learned and developed these practices from conversations with every single client, participant and colleague. We hope that our never-ending curiosity on the question, "What is the simplest way to get the best from everyone, everywhere, anytime?" may inspire you to put our proven practices into action.

Thank you to all our mentors and masters, who were a continuous source of inspiration and shared their wisdom with us in personal conversations, workshops and writings throughout the years.

We would like to see our practices become more and more commonly used in people's work and in their personal lives. In the end it's all about a genuine people-centric approach. Please accept and enjoy this book as our two cents worth on how to build a better world.

Dirk Devos
Manon de Wit
Robert Lubberding

It is not the strongest of
the species that survives
but the most adaptable.

paraphrased from Charles Darwin
by Megginson

WHY THIS BOOK IS IMPORTANT

There is no way back. Change is physical and turbulent in the social and political aspects of life, in business and in the day-to-day lives of ordinary people. Existing structures are being dismantled; new ways of 'coopetition' within and between ecosystems are being reshaped. The only option is to be adaptive and have the ability to create the best from what is possible.

In order to become increasingly adaptive in society, a genuine people-centric approach is required.

To make this a reality, we need to get the best from everyone, everywhere, anytime.

So how can we shift the needle from where we are today to where we want to be?

To do this effectively we must let go of thinking in terms of 'human resources' – in the sense of looking at people as though they are raw materials – and open our minds to gain a better and a deeper understanding of what makes people tick as individuals and collectively in a group.

A MORE GRANULAR UNDERSTANDING OF PEOPLE

People are born and raised in family settings that help shape their personal internal views and their social dialogues in life. The groups and relationships that people live in can activate their best and their worst attributes.

Organizations are social webs of networked conversations governed by explicit and implicit rules of agreement. That is how we shape the dialogic infrastructure.

Meetings are gatherings where views and ideas are exchanged to find common resolutions. These discussions enable organizations to progress and move forward. Meetings are also places where we act out our personal need to be seen, to be heard, and to be valued for who we really are and what we bring to the table. Meetings are the perfect place to act out dominance and navigate or fight conflicts in the hope that we will finally accomplish our goals.

On a daily basis at work, we find that our calendars are tightly packed with back-to-back meetings. We find ourselves sitting in energy draining conference rooms, at large tables where we often repeat unproductive and dysfunctional rituals of the past.

As a consequence, invisible human boundaries, both intrapersonal and interpersonal, develop and grow into systemic boundaries that are recognized in business as organizational silos. These can break down the structural webs of meaningful conversations in the dialogic infrastructure. Therefore, anxieties arise and block a people-centric approach. In this process, we find that we lose our sense of curiosity and exploration, which prevents us from becoming more adaptive.

Recent research[1] has identified two core drivers that are critical to an organization's development: building trusted relationships and fostering an ongoing, collective process of redefining meaning. This is called 'fostering generative relationships'. With an increase in organizational complexities and mounting anxiety, we see a breakdown of relationships and the capacity for collective strategizing gets lost.

Most of us handle and cope with difficult group dynamics intuitively. We apply automatic reflexes and repeat familiar patterns of behaviour to navigate the ups and downs experienced in groups and elsewhere in the organization. Sometimes it works, sometimes it does not. Think metaphorically of the latest software applications running on an outdated operating system, and the havoc wreaked by the inevitable system crashes.

We believe that it's time to upgrade our conscious understanding from a command and control mindset to one of 'leading from behind'. Not just to talk about it, but to truly shift our daily practices so that we start setting the right example in leading from behind.

Those who are exceptional
at leading from behind are likely
to be different than those who
excelled at leading from the front.
And this raises the question:
are we identifying and developing
the leaders who can tap the power
of the collective genius?

Linda A. Hill

SHIFTING THE NEEDLE

To accomplish the shift towards leading from behind, we need a powerful key to radically transform the effectiveness of our organization's internal dialogue. Based on tens of thousands of conversations, we've distilled nine human business transformation practices that together form the Leading from Behind practice model. Although these nine practices are supported by theory, they have emerged from real-world practice and have proven to be highly effective. They are simple, yet powerful. Each of these practices promises passionate collective energy, exponential acceleration and robust business impact. How? Through getting the best from everyone, everywhere, anytime.

Above all, the nine practices generate massive amounts of extra time. Why? Because they significantly reduce the nonsense, the energy draining activities, the misalignments, the miscommunications and the dysfunctions that exist in organizations when individuals try to work collaboratively.

At first, the logical structure of the model may not seem obvious and, for this reason, we invite you to explore the irrational, non-linear power of the Leading from Behind practice model. Nonetheless, the true power of people-centric adaptive transformation resides in this irrational domain. Rationality is only a minute fraction of our human power. In fact, what we believe in – and the role models we see in action – help shape our world. If we want to become

more adaptive, we need to change our beliefs about how people are motivated. Until now we have been educated by previous generations of leaders and therefore copied many of their beliefs and behaviours in our attempts to drive transformational change. But the problem is that many of these beliefs and practices are not effective any more.

In the following chapters you'll find a description of the nine practices, which will rapidly help to shift the needle to a more desirable place. These practices require rigorous application and wider multiplication through role-modelling. To get the best from everyone, everywhere, anytime. Let's get started.

WHAT GREAT COULD LOOK LIKE

IMAGINE...

... Your leaders are inclusive and invite the right people with the right talent to the meeting.

... Every meeting starts with a powerful question to address the real key challenges.

... Every meeting is all about getting the best from you and your colleagues.

... You can trust the team when the heat is on.

... You continuously get the full energy of everyone on the team.

... Everyone has the power to regulate their emotions when the pressure is high.

... You can reset your mind, kill your limiting beliefs and open up to grow as a leader.

... The drive of your personal purpose, values and vision directly feeds into the organization.

... You have the power of courageous conversations to bring clear resolve and swift decisions.

... The whole team coaches each other with continuous feedback/feedforward.

... You turn your anxiety into courage and do what you have to do for the good.

Getting the best from everyone, everywhere, anytime is not that complicated. It's a choice.

LEADING FROM BEHIND PRACTICE MODEL

Working with others

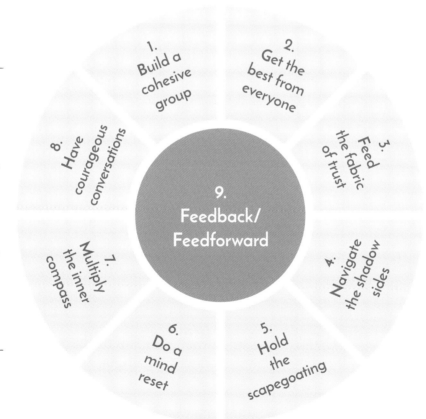

Working with our light sides

Working with our shadow sides

1. Build a cohesive group

2. Get the best from everyone

3. Feed the fabric of trust

4. Navigate the shadow sides

5. Hold the scapegoating

6. Do a mind reset

7. Multiply the inner compass

8. Have courageous conversations

9. Feedback/ Feedforward

Working with our inner self

HOW TO USE THE LEADING FROM BEHIND PRACTICE MODEL

The Leading from Behind practice model is built around two structural tensions, with nine practice sections to help navigate them. They lay out a concise, replicable model that – when thoughtfully applied – will help reduce anxiety, build courage and increase role-modelling within a team.

In any role, at any point in time, in any context, a leader faces two areas: the inner self versus relationships with others. In these there are two types of forces at play: our light sides and our shadow sides. The light side encompasses our positive, constructive beliefs, values and behaviours; the shadow side comprises our negative, destructive, dysfunctional beliefs, values and behaviours.

When we come to the core essence of leading transformation, these are the ultimate forces that all leaders use and operate within. And it is our belief that while there is a need for individual leadership we also need collective leadership from all the members in the team.

We can start the transformation process with practice 1, Build a Cohesive Group, and sequentially navigate through the model to practice 9, Feedback/Feedforward. Or one can take a deep dive into a practice that is relevant for a specific group at a specific moment in time. Ideally, we would recommend that users explore the model and start from where they feel would be most suitable for the people on their team – a blended approach.

Build a Cohesive Team

1. BUILD A COHESIVE TEAM

SHAPING A HEALTHY INTEGRATED TEAM

Human systems do not like change. As a rule, we like to stay in our comfort zone and stick with the familiar. We prefer to keep doing more of the same, rather than integrating differences to differentiate, stretch and become more adaptive. This is deeply ingrained in our DNA and consists of three states:[2]

- **Our curious self** – the life force that decides to include and integrate differences.
- **Our repetitive self** – the need to look for similarities.
- **Our explorative self** – the desire to actively search for differences.

When they're out of their comfort zones, people experience rising levels of anxiety and erect invisible boundaries with other members of the group. These boundaries change the individual's ability to use their personal power, curiosity and adaptive exploration and prompt them to reinforce their routine behaviour.

It is these invisible boundaries that create divisions within groups. When this pattern repeats and multiplies it can generate organizational fragmentation – one of the most stubborn impediments to structurally and collectively getting the best from everyone in any organization.

Unity is what is required to reduce the anxieties of individuals and subsequently reduce conflicts between members of the group. Unity is therefore essential for individuals and groups to co-evolve and adapt in a rapidly changing world.

There are three systemic laws for social systems that must be appreciated in order to build organizational unity. In short, these come together and form 'BOB':[3]

- Bonding – inclusion/exclusion.
- Order – respecting the natural ranking/hierarchy.
- Balance – equilibrium in give and take.

Unity within an organization results from designing and building an internal system for dialogue that prevents ongoing fragmentation as much as possible.

Every individual wants to experience a sense of belonging and every social group is defined by its own rules of 'inclusion' and 'exclusion'. Inclusion means ensuring that the right people are participating in the appropriate circles to talk through the relevant issues. Exclusion leads to structural boundaries that build invisible walls separating people, teams and groups. This, in turn, causes structural fragmentation, which is experienced as organizational silos.

A fundamental requirement for preventing such breakdown in an organization is having respect for the 'ranking order'. This requires respect for the key people, the hierarchy, the culture, the iconic moments, the rituals and the achievements as a precondition for plotting a course into the future.

Whenever there is an imbalance in give and take, the organization will suffer from fragmentation.

Intense courage is required to design an organization – its decision-making processes and the actions it takes in pursuit of change – in a way that pays ultimate respect to the three fundamental laws of social structures: bonding, order and balance.

In a world of intermeshed ecosystems, where ambiguity and complexity levels are even higher, the impact of the above principles is even greater. Who is in? Who is out? Who has which role in the value chain? How can we maintain the balance of give and take? These questions are crucial to the continuity, effectiveness and value creation in the network.

In any organization, encouraging teamwork when addressing powerful questions is a highly effective way to build a cohesive group that takes ownership.

When Einstein was asked what he would do if he had to solve a complex problem in 60 minutes, he answered: "I would spend 55 minutes identifying the most powerful question that would help solve the problem. Then I would try to find the answer in the remaining five minutes." Similarly, one of the most powerful interventions for leaders is spending more time and paying closer attention to formulating the most powerful questions, and then mobilizing their teams to collaboratively find the best answers.

The optimal dialogue structure is in sync with the following priorities for the leader:

- Are we working on the right, most powerful question to be resolved?
- Are the right people who can address this question sitting in the room?
- Are we getting the best from everyone in the room?

CASE STUDY:
'BUILD A COHESIVE TEAM'

An international financial services company had been struggling for some time to find a strategic breakthrough in its digital banking initiatives. The challenge was to find a solution that would enable potential new clients to instantly contract a loan via their mobile phones. However, the underlying complexity of banking regulations and legacy technology were significant barriers.

Together with the company's senior leaders we addressed the need for a powerful leading question and asked what that should be. A powerful leading question is open and starts with why, how or what. It helps the group explain the root causes by hindsight or explore the path forward. The leader's role is to reflect and shape a question most relevant and helpful for the team to find its way. The next step was to identify and invite the people with the talent to answer this question to a special meeting. To do this effectively they needed to look for talent outside of their own departments, while also considering individuals who had been working on this challenge for a long time.

Irrespective of loyalties, it was important not to invite people out of courtesy. When the new people began contributing to the discussion, it soon became clear how much more information, insights and partial solutions had already been developed in different pockets of the organization. From the original list of invitees, more than a third of the participants were replaced by others with the right talent.

So that each participant could prepare, all insights and information were consolidated into one exhaustive package and disseminated before the meeting. The leading questions for the meeting were also shared in advance, so that everyone could prepare their own thoughts. During the meeting, there were no PowerPoint slides and, in fact, no presentations of any sort. After a one-hour team building exercise with a group of 16 participants – in which many people met each other for the first time – they were asked to take a few minutes and reflect on the leading questions. Then the participants were asked to pair up and go for a walk, sharing their thoughts and consolidating their insights, thoughts and suggestions. At the end of this exercise, it became clear that each small group had proposals that could be combined into an overall approach to solve the problem. In effect, the team had collectively designed a high-level roadmap. In only four hours, this cross-functional group, that had never met before, achieved a major breakthrough.

Get the Best from Everyone

2. GET THE BEST FROM EVERYONE

HOW TO GET PEOPLE TO CONSTANTLY GIVE THEIR BEST

Once the right group of people are in the room, ready to share their talent and collaboratively resolve the powerful leading question, then it's time to get the best from everyone. This requires a deeper understanding of team dynamics and awareness of your own role within these dynamics. It starts with striking a balance between four leadership behaviours[4] in action:

- **Move** ... to provide ideas on where to go and direction on how to get there.
- **Follow** ... to build upon proposed ideas and build momentum for execution.
- **Oppose** ... to correct and challenge proposed ideas in order to ensure quality.
- **Bystand** ... to provide perspective for the group.

Top-down leadership makes it difficult to obtain this dynamic balance. Yet, great leaders have the ability to unlock the collective intelligence of the group. They 'get out of the way' and let their teams create extraordinary outcomes. As a result, the individuals and the team feel more ownership and responsibility. Individuals grow in self-esteem, and the trust and 'can do' mentality among team members increases.

This is important because large organizations want to shift from a 'command and control' style of leadership towards an 'adaptive/agile' one. Accountability and resources are delegated to people deep within the organization so that they can focus on customer centricity, innovation and value creation.

A consequence of top-down leadership is that this style is copied across the organization. With this construct, the value chain of human attention is bottom-up – people give their superiors more attention than their fellow team members, hoping that the leaders will see, hear and value them.

If we really want to become adaptive, it is imperative that we invert the chain of attention: leaders coach leaders, who coach their team members, who in turn coach their clients, their ecosystem partners and their colleagues. That is the essence of leading from behind.

As many of us have been taught, leadership is all about 'knowing it all', 'showing them the way' and 'explaining how to get there'. Conversely, leading from behind is all about maximizing the power of collective leadership, which requires a balanced group dynamic.

Leading from behind demands that leaders pay attention to this strong tendency to Move and provide their team with direction. Recommendations for improved behaviour include: talk less, ask powerful open questions and speak last. Slow down to go faster!

Leading from behind actually requires:

- **Followership:** a coaching style of leading that encourages and provides emotional support to other team members so that they can take ownership and move things forward.

- **Challenging:** asking powerful, genuine, open questions while respecting others' perspectives.
- **Observing:** actively providing feedback/feedforward that helps others find a common way forward.

Feedback is looking backwards, making the person reflect on his or her behaviour and its impact. The benefit is that it shapes the conditions for having a courageous conversation. The risk is that a team ends up turning in circles and going back to square one. Feedback can best be applied when we want to eliminate a dysfunctional pattern.

Feedforward is shaping perspectives from the present into the future, while expressing the behaviour you would like to see and exploring what is needed for that. The benefit is that the team jointly shapes the conditions and collaboratively creates a desired path forward. The risk is in not addressing destructive patterns. Feedforward can best be applied when we want to accelerate a common path forward.

The key lesson for leaders who want to improve is to stop providing the group with ideas and proposals. If leaders continually focus on laying out their own thoughts and perspectives, and direct their team along those lines, they stand in the way of the group taking ownership. By doing so leaders will continue to block their teams and inhibit their pursuit of a common path forward.

Ultimately, a group needs a good, equal balance[5,6] of advocacy and inquiry.

Advocacy is characterized by an intensive and repetitive Move-Oppose dynamic (ideas and direction vis-à-vis challenges) in the form of critical discussions. When discussions increase tensions, people passively Follow and Bystand by withdrawing from the heated conversation.

Fewer and fewer people will remain actively involved in the conversation as anxiety levels increase. Being able and willing to hold a heated conversation without letting it escalate is crucial. Turning the conversation into an inquiry is the best way to expand on these discussions and take a positive step forward.

An inquiry is characterized by asking powerful open questions with an appreciative intention that generates an active, intensive and repetitive Follow-Bystand dynamic (giving feedback/feedforward while building positive momentum).

In an inquiry like this, where open questions are posed, tensions decrease and the mood of the conversation becomes broader again as the group's anxiety levels decrease. Asking powerful open questions is key to progression.

Being successful in the four leadership behaviours requires four corresponding qualities:[5,19]

- **A good voice quality**, for Move to clearly express the proposed direction.
- **Deep, intensive listening**, for Follow to understand the proposed directions by Move, as well as the challenges from Oppose and the perspectives from Bystand.
- **Respect for the differences**, for Oppose to maintain good levels of trust.
- **Suspending judgment**, for Bystand to keep an open mind.

Leading from behind is a powerful way to create optimal conditions for the three systemic requirements mentioned: bonding, order and balance. It also enables leaders to invite everyone to offer their best contributions to the conversation so that the group itself can transform its existing collective stories and beliefs into ones that are refreshing and new.

Leading from behind increases the passion for continuous renewal. As a result, there is less anxiety as people become more comfortable and believe in the new vision and direction of the team.

Leading from behind multiplies the sense of ownership across the entire organization as people take ownership of what they believe in and can create themselves.

CASE STUDY: 'GET THE BEST FROM EVERYONE'

The leader of an international group of finance professionals was confronted with troubling feedback about his leadership style. The overall feedback was that he acted like a super expert and always wanted to have the last say. His people felt intimidated, and a number of them resigned. None of the team members felt empowered and they didn't dare oppose the executive's point of view.

The leader was offered corrective coaching to help resolve the situation. During this process he committed to making a radical change: he would adopt an entirely different leadership style. Instead of leading from the front – where there's a great need for control, such as setting direction and micromanaging – he would lead from behind. This would entail guiding the group by asking questions and inviting people to surface their best ideas, take personal initiative and seize ownership through collaborative decision-making. The coaching helped this leader explore, unravel and reshape the behavioural patterns, underlying beliefs, root causes and emotions that fuelled his dysfunctional behaviour.

One of the first steps this executive took was to invite his management team to an offsite retreat, characterized as a 'leadership journey'. The three-day getaway in the mountains was intended to create a new foundation for the team. The idea was received with scepticism, as the trust level in the organization was quite low and people doubted the leader's intentions.

During the trip the leader opened up and shared with his managers the impact the transformational journey had on him. He explained how he'd underestimated the impact of his leadership style on the people around him, and that he wanted to regain their confidence. He invited all team members to support him in his personal transformation and asked for help in creating better overall team performance.

The retreat was a blend of hiking, talking and periods of silence. The process was built around inquiry and self-reflection, beginning with powerful guiding questions. Participants were encouraged to share insights and experiences and be truthful about their emotions. They spoke about how the

intimidating, toxic workplace had impacted them, the nature of their relationships and how they wanted to move forward through collaboration within the organization. Participants shared personal experiences, which helped to bring them closer together and led to further courageous discussions about the way the group was organized and how members could better fulfil their roles.

For a few, the process led to a realization that they didn't want to travel the road the team had chosen, and they decided to leave the company.

This leadership journey served as a catalyst for strategic business discussions and team initiatives on exceeding customer expectations, clarity in roles and responsibilities and better use of the company's international resources, as well as developing a feedback/feedforward culture. These initiatives were set up in a way that reflected the core leading from behind principles, and involved managers coaching each other while realizing their own personal ambitions.

Feed the Fabric of Trust

3. FEED THE FABRIC OF TRUST

CREATING A SAFE AND TRUSTING ENVIRONMENT

Trust is one of the most talked about themes within organizations. Many people express their desire for a higher level of trust, and hope that teambuilding sessions and leadership development programmes will help nurture that trust. Retreats, coaching and professional development courses can help, but they aren't a magic bullet. Why is this the case? Because deeper layers of anxiety just don't get addressed, and staying too polite in the safe (easy) zone does nothing to build trust.

One of the key roles of senior leaders is to reduce anxiety and create an environment of trust, where people can deliver their best. Trust is a result – an outcome from an ongoing process. To build and reinforce the fabric of trust requires a systematic process. It starts with understanding the dynamics of anxieties within the team and learning how to shift them, both across the group and at a personal level. Anything that does not address this in depth will not work in the long run.

During business conversations, team members act out their anxieties, which have three different sources. These are: scary thoughts, scary feelings and being at the edge of the unknown.[2] Anxieties develop when colleagues'

opinions begin to diverge too dramatically. One of the biggest challenges facing teams is how they deal with differences. This crucial openness to alternate views requires people to slow down and embrace differences when the team is strong and can find a way to integrate such differences. Scary thoughts[2] are acted out in the form of negative predictions and mind-reads. Both have a significant negative impact on feeling safe within the group and its general 'can-do mentality'.

Undoing negative predictions[2] is the role of each team member, and of the team leader in particular. To undo a negative prediction requires a group to first explore the context in the form of functional subgrouping. Focus on the first major difference in the group, only invite those to speak who agree with a specific point of view and let everybody speak truthfully and let all their opinions emerge. Next, invite everyone who disagrees to provide their point of view. Then synergize and synthesize, before moving on and applying the same process to the next major difference in the group.

To clarify the negative prediction, a team member can ask the person who expressed it the following question: "Can you predict the future?" In most cases the person will smile and relax, and the team can move on. If not, the group should be supportive in exploring the differences and underlying assumptions instead of reacting negatively or shutting down the pessimistic thinkers.

Undoing mind-reads[2] requires asking colleagues to share their assumptions openly in the group. It's as simple as saying, "John, it appears that you believe [...]. Is that right?"

It is also important to detect scary feelings[2] in the group, which can cause tense feelings, apprehensive thoughts and unpleasant sensations in the body, like changes in breathing, stomach, bowels, heart, throat or limbs. It is the role of each team member, and especially the leader, to regularly check in with the team to see how people are feeling, to invite them to express their feelings.

People can also experience anxiety because they are at the edge of the unknown.[2] The key is how they can change their anxiety into curiosity. This requires turning your critical mind into an open mind.

Humans have a survival system. We build this during our childhood and project our learnings into the here and now. At a personal level, five universal anxieties[7] have been identified: injustice, betrayal, humiliation, abandonment and rejection. Each person in any group may have one, several or all of these deep-seated anxieties, which lurk as hidden triggers that can be activated in a split second. To prevent themselves from repeatedly being hurt, over time people build defensive behavioural mechanisms, which may range from rigidity and control to servility, dependency and withdrawal.

At times of vulnerability, every person longs to be seen, heard and sympathetically embraced. Depending on what triggers them, people yearn for transparency, pro-active trust, appreciation, inclusion and intimacy. These reduce people's anxieties and restore their capacity for constructive collaboration. In this respect, it's imperative that leaders imbue the organization with transparency, pro-active trust, appreciation, inclusion and intimacy.

Analysis of employee engagement surveys confirms that this is exactly what people are longing for. By providing the group with what it needs to feed the fabric of trust, leaders ensure that they are getting the best from each individual. The leader can and should encourage this by setting the example.

The 'Law of Santa Claus' is one of the most powerful techniques for getting unstuck when anxieties arise. The name comes from the idea that if you put something on your wish list, there is a good chance of getting it. In short, this technique involves asking explicitly, nicely and honestly with a clear voice, for the transparency, pro-active trust, appreciation, inclusion and intimacy one craves. By simply expressing your desires, there's a good chance that you'll receive what you need at a difficult time.

As a leader, you'll find that it is good practice to ask your people what they need when they're under pressure. Likewise, a leader should ask team members to provide what is needed when the pressure is on.

The more we reveal about ourselves, the more others will get to know us in different ways, the more reliable we will become, and the more trust there will be.

CASE STUDY:
'FEED THE FABRIC OF TRUST'

The newly appointed Chief Human Resources Officer (CHRO) of a multinational industrial production company was asked to transform the locally organized HR community into a solid team of partners who would help facilitate the organization's major transformations.

He carefully selected key players in the global HR community and invited them to embark on a leadership journey to transform the function. He was convinced that this group would be able to co-create the future HR playbook, knowing that this process would also be transformational for each of the key players themselves.

Together with the CHRO, we designed an experiential learning journey, consisting of several workshops.

We started with a process of personal and professional bonding by getting to know each other beyond the company roles and understanding the context of each local HR practice. The key players formulated and shared their individual purpose, values and vision, and co-created a shared vision for the future of HR.

A deep dive into each team member's vulnerabilities and defence mechanisms helped forge the professional intimacy and interpersonal chemistry necessary to address and undo negative thoughts and feelings. People really opened up. As a consequence, the willingness and intensity to further explore new paths in the HR transformation process increased significantly. In the end, this approach compelled participants to take ownership of the key themes and issues that were critical to achieving the vision.

The CHRO ensured that the process was inclusive and encouraged each team member to participate and contribute. We guided courageous conversations where fundamental issues with high personal impact were discussed and resolved. The non-judgmental way in which the dialogue was facilitated allowed participants to share their personal worries and strengthened the bonding and trust created at the start of the transformation process. Through this reckoning process several colleagues came to understand that the new direction would not fit with their personal purpose and capabilities. And although they left the company, the way these personal issues were handled contributed to the credibility of the chosen vision and strengthened the values of the HR function.

Navigate the Shadow Sides

4. NAVIGATE THE SHADOW SIDES

ACKNOWLEDGING, AND USING, OUR DARKER FORCES

The shadow side encompasses our negative, destructive, dysfunctional beliefs, values and behaviours.

As our personal and professional lives become ever more complex and challenging, our shadow sides reveal that rationality cannot keep up. More and more conversations become irrational and we ask our intuition to act as an internal data screener. As a result, our dialogues become fuzzy, erratic and iterative. This triggers a nagging sense of uncertainty and doubt, which lead to shadow side behaviour when we work in groups.

Whenever the space is not safe – when the three systemic laws of bonding-order-balance are not respected, or leading from behind is not applied – our shadow sides are at play. Yet, it's worth noting that in addition to the destructive forces seen in our shadow sides, beneficial forces also reside there. It is the leader's role to maximize the value that the team can get from the power of the shadows while reducing negative impacts. That requires the leader to reduce anxiety levels, which, in turn, leads to a greater sense of safety. And with that, the team is more likely to give its best at work.

Shadow sides are activated in different ways, and take on various forms and shapes. They may be prompted by intense Move-Oppose dynamics, which increase anxiety and trigger withdrawal and passive Bystander and Follower behaviours.

When these tensions rise, people become critically sensitive to the type of language[5] that is used: the language of the mind (understanding), the heart (feeling) or the body (doing). Conflicts may emerge when people who prefer the language of the mind need more time to get their head around it, while those who prefer the language of the gut grow impatient for immediate action. In this tension, people who prefer the language of the heart may feel pushed aside ('no time for feelings now').

At a deeper level, our systemic preferences[4] for 'structure', 'inclusion' or 'freedom' have a major impact on us when we are working under pressure. Essential structure-structure and structure-freedom tensions between people with these corresponding preferences may cause fights and slow down or even paralyze the team's performance. Dominance of the freedom preference (having the free space to do what you believe is right) is perceived as chaotic, while dominance of the structure preference (having structural control over what you believe is right) is experienced as overly hierarchical. Meanwhile, dominance of the inclusion preference may cause a tyranny of process paralysis.

When the heat is on, we get both the best and the worst of people. The following three archetypes[4] can help us better understand the behaviours in a team:

- **Fixers** solve problems, while causing collateral damage as they push others aside.
- **Survivors** choose their battles with a high capacity for endurance, but withdraw when the tension becomes too intense.

- **Protectors** fight against adversity when values, causes or relationships are perceived to be endangered, while blaming themselves and others.

We should not forget that our shadow sides are the innate forces that give us the ambition, energy and drive needed to move mountains. The more intense the shadow sides are, the stronger the drive to succeed, although this also presents a greater risk of group dysfunction.

Teams require a proper sense of safety to do their work. The core work of the team[2] is to find commonalities, explore differences and integrate them. That is why personal, interpersonal and system boundaries need to be semi-permeable, so that differences can pass through and introduce diversity, which is key to becoming adaptive. Once commonalities are found the team can move on to the next level of the conversation. From there, the process is repeated in order to find commonalities, explore and integrate the differences.

Exploring and integrating our differences requires holding the power of our shadows within clear and safe team boundaries. Starting with appreciation is key. If people are not heard and seen for who they truly are, and what they bring to the table, this will automatically activate the shadow side. A powerful approach is to continually 'Celebrate what is right, and have the energy to fix what is wrong'.[8]

It is the role of the leader to assure the right levels of safety so the team can do its work. This requires positive intent, emotional maturity, presence and consciousness, as well as a deep understanding of one's life and experiences with personal transformation. The latter is important, as it helps regulate one's hidden triggers and defence mechanisms. In this way, the leader can remain grounded and calmly engaged during difficult times and prevent the team from breaking up or reverting to a state of distant politeness.[5,9]

A key role for the leader is to use the power of the shadow sides in the group to help team members wrestle through the mess. An effective way to navigate forward is through asking powerful, open, feed-forward questions.[5,6,9] Feed-forward questions are those that help the team explore its way forward. A pre-condition for all of this is that the first three steps are well worked through: build a cohesive team, get the best from everyone and feed the fabric of trust.

CASE STUDY:
'NAVIGATE THE SHADOW SIDES'

The executive board of an international power company had nine members. They wanted to improve their team effectiveness and especially fix their less-than-productive board meetings. They agreed that when they were all together, they were rather dysfunctional.

When this senior team did a self-diagnosis and feedback scan (see practice: 'Get the best from everyone'), eight out of nine were identified in Move, with one person in Bystand. No wonder the board meetings were difficult – everyone was speaking their own voice and constantly making proposals to the group on where to go and how to get there. They often found themselves pointing in different directions. And one person (the 'Bystander') was always left out and did not have the tenacity to change these powerful dynamics.

This extraordinary tension activated the next communication level. When the pressure increases, we have specific language preferences that may cause great irritation: the language of the mind (Understanding), the heart (Feeling), and the body (Action). Six of the nine team members were identified in Action, and three in Understanding. And so, in a team of nine,

eight were making proposals in different directions, and when they could not reach an agreement six of them became so impatient that they felt they urgently needed to get into action mode and do something to get things moving. Meanwhile, the other three needed more time to get their heads around it all before they could take another step.

This tension between impatience for action versus needing more time for thinking triggered the next communication level, where five of them desperately wanted a more structured approach, albeit differing on what that entailed and not being open to each other's perspectives.

And four of them had a strong freedom preference, with a hard wired preference for space, latitude and working in an emergent way. They hated to be put in boxes by the people with the structured profile, who in turn got mad about what they saw as chaotic randomness.

This then activated the next communication level, with six people exhibiting a Fixer profile and three a Protector profile. This triggered intense fights until the chairman called for order, trying to steer things back to a reasonably polite conversation. Unfortunately, they missed the opportunity to wrestle through the mess in order to get to the next level – a more explorative and collaborative conversation.

Sadly, this pattern had been evolving in the company's senior executive ranks for years.

Dysfunctional behaviour was on full display in the boardroom: fragmentation, blaming, power abuse, negative predictions and mind reading. Along the way, team members internalized negative feelings, and that activated their defence mechanisms: rigidity, control, servile conduct, dependency and withdrawal.

The intervention that turned this situation around had three fundamental building blocks:

1. Work to significantly improve communication at the first two levels (Level 1: Move/Follow/Oppose/Bystand; Level2: Understanding/Feeling/Action). This was necessary to avoid getting trapped in the dynamics of levels three and four (Level 3: Structure/Open/Freedom; Level 4: Fixer/Survivor/Protector). Team members were urged to balance expressing their personal voice versus asking powerful questions that could help the team to move forward. When speaking, they were encouraged to build upon what was said by others. This required extreme discipline from each participant, but everybody knew for sure that if they didn't change they could not continue as a team.

2. In the heat of the moment, undo negative predictions (can you predict the future?) and mind reads (check assumptions) in the team meetings.

3. Direct meetings with powerful leading questions. A well-informed, meaningful boardroom conversation depended on providing the team with relevant information beforehand. That would drive good conversations and get the best contribution from everyone, instead of bogging down in the old information download followed by a dysfunctional debate. How did it work out? When properly coached, the team was very disciplined and on a scale of 1-10 it moved from a weak 2 to a dramatically more collaborative 7. After six months of coaching, they had a structural improvement reaching a 5. Not perfect, but a major step forward.

Hold the Scapegoating

5. HOLD THE SCAPEGOATING

HARNESSING AND SMOOTHENING THE TENSION

It takes a huge amount of energy and determination to grow into a senior leader role. And one could argue that it takes even more energy to stay in that position, since pressure comes from all sides: financial markets, customers, competition, the ecosystem and value chain partners, supervisory boards, board colleagues, bottom-up from the organization, etc.

Another measure of leadership is the capacity to harness the tension and cope with ongoing, multiple attacks from all stakeholders, and from team members in particular, who are projecting[2] their hopes and fears onto the leader. Leaders need tremendous stamina to navigate the stormy weather. True mastery of leadership involves getting in touch with the feelings that are triggered by attacks from others. This is a recurring group dynamic phenomenon that cannot be avoided. People bring their life experiences, vulnerabilities and defensive behaviour into every conversation. They subconsciously yearn to be seen, heard and valued. They hope their leader will provide them with the five solutions: transparency, trust, appreciation, inclusion and intimacy. Their deepest wish is for the leader to heal their wounds from the past. People have this very strong implicit expectation

that leaders will take care of them, almost taking on the role of their parents.

It puts a lot of emotional pressure on the leader to control his shadows and not allow them to become activated following such attacks. To be seen as a beacon of safety, a leader must possess self-knowledge, a clear inner compass, an appreciative mindset, emotional self-regulation and compassion for others. Many of today's leaders have been educated through role-modelling by parents, teachers, early career managers and other leaders. As a result, an organization can expose people to varying levels of consciousness and practice capabilities on a daily basis.

It's assumed that leaders must have strong shadows if they've demonstrated the energy and drive necessary to get to where they are, and to stay there while driving the organization forward. At the same time, they need to be able to contain all the pressure of scapegoating without losing ground and self-confidence. Such pressures activate the leader's shadow sides and corresponding defensive behaviour.[2] This is counterproductive for the individuals in the team: as tension increases, their yearning deepens for transparency, trust, appreciation, inclusion and intimacy. This process, playing out in the pressure cooker of organizational tension, increases the distance between leaders and their people and is one of the root causes of continuous fragmentation in our organizations. It is important, both for the leader and the team members, to not take it personally. They must recognize that scapegoating is part of the team dynamics process, and it's actually necessary if the leader and the group hope to reach the next level. Transformational success demands that a leader deal with it and, with a warm heart, redirect and transform this scapegoating tension into a constructive context for team learning.

This is why it is so important for all of our leaders to continuously work on their consciousness, mindset, beliefs, behaviours and deeper personal shadows: to become a bigger human being, to become a bigger leader, to grow a bigger business. This can serve as an important starting point for leadership from the inside-out, whereby role-modelling is the ultimate multiplier for collective leadership.

The real work we have to do is the inner work. This calls for not blindly following our primary impulses when under pressure, but staying tuned in, regulating our emotions and supporting the team's growth and forward movement with warmth and understanding. This inner work consists of doing a mind reset, labouring through emotional transformation on unresolved issues, applying breathing techniques to regulate emotions in the heat of the moment and meditation to improve one's presence.[9,10]

It is painful to see many leaders, and others throughout an organization, looking upward and projecting their frustrations and wishes onto their CEO and board members. Instead, they could be shaping their own organizational community movement and doing what they can themselves. We expect our senior leaders to be 'superhuman', but they are not. They have strong shadows and they're trying to grow as they go along. Instead of looking upward, leaders need to trust their good intent, refocus on those they lead and put the time and effort into coaching and mentoring their people.

Of course, leaders will often point a finger at the dysfunctional behaviour of the CEO and his board members. And, inevitably, they will suffer for it, at a personal level, in their teams and in the business as a whole.

Embrace the notion that if we want to change the world, it's best to start with ourselves and then build a small group of people to role-model and drive the change we want to see. "Never doubt that a small group … can change the world. Indeed, it is the only thing that ever has."[11]

Becoming a transformational leader requires a deep mind reset, where leaders can learn how to internally 'connect the dots' between their life story and their leadership story. This will allow them to unlearn some of the old beliefs that are blocking their leadership practices. In the end, the real work we need to do is the inner work.

CASE STUDY:
'HOLD THE SCAPEGOATING'

After ten years as the number-two executive at a fast-moving consumer goods (FMCG) company, the senior leader stepped into the CEO role. It was not easy to fill the shoes of his predecessor, who had strongly run the huge, global company for more than 20 years. Although the former leader's charismatic personality was a source of pride within the company, it was having a hard time holding its top-three position in the industry. It was clear that a new strategy was needed. Perhaps more importantly, it had become apparent that the organization needed an entirely new way of working.

In the tradition of the previous CEO, the new leader held a workshop to engage in the necessary strategic dialogue. The session was prepared and facilitated by an external consultant who had worked with this group for the previous decade. During that session, the group's demeanour was very different from before; the atmosphere was one of low engagement, low commitment, harsh critiquing and negative energy. Things, in fact, became so bad that the meeting was stopped half way through and the group was promised a follow-up session two months later.

The design and planning for this new workshop was completely different. Participants were intensively interviewed to collect their insights and beliefs about strategy, business and organizational issues, as well as collective and individual leadership. Following these interviews, small groups were invited to work on specific strategic challenges. They would then share their findings and recommendations in the larger meeting. In parallel, the CEO and the board of directors prepared their perspectives and built alignment and ownership, leaving space for their ideas to be challenged by the individual work groups.

The meeting started off well enough. But then, barely a third of the way in, the proceedings took a dark turn, just as they had in the initial workshop. The group started to blame the new CEO. As much as they liked him when he was second in command, now they collectively projected their fears and frustrations onto him. Certainly, the group wanted to test their new chief executive. But also, at a deeper level, the strategizing process heightened their anxiety levels. Some saw the leadership transition as an opportunity to drive their own vision and agenda forward. And so, along with their fears and frustrations, they also projected their aspirations, hopes and desires onto the new CEO.

The CEO experienced a huge amount of pressure from the group. He reacted by becoming more and more dominant and assuming more control, which, in turn, intensified the blaming by the group. All of this happened in only a few minutes.

Ultimately, the CEO's thorough personal preparation paid off. As the blame and recrimination flew, he self-regulated his strong emotions, slowly took three deep breaths and changed his tone of voice. In a friendly way he asked a powerful question: "Our communication has taken on a very hostile tone. What is it that we need as a group to turn this into a more positive experience?" He then asked everyone in the room to take a few minutes to reflect on themselves – what they were thinking, feeling and saying – and on the group process. It was only then that everyone calmed down, opened up and voiced their personal truth. The atmosphere shifted to a better place, and the group started to do the real work.

Do a
Mind
Reset

6. DO A MIND RESET

TRANSFORMING INGRAINED THOUGHT PATTERNS

As a leader, we endeavour to bring our best to the business. Behavioural science tells us that 60% of our character is attributable to DNA. The other 40% in the nature/nurture equation is what we've copied and learned from our parents, family, friends, teachers, managers and significant life experiences that has shaped the beliefs that drive our behaviour. When we want to change the way we fit into an adaptive culture in a complex world, we need to change some of the beliefs that previously brought us success. "What brought you here won't bring you there."[12] We need a mindset that keeps using what we already have that's good and helpful, as well as resetting a few deeply held beliefs in order to progress to the next level of success.

We all know this situation: new leader, new top structure, new appointments. All of these are intended to put the right teams in the right positions to move towards breakthrough success. The plan, if we were to mine the vast lexicon of corporate clichés here, will be to become agile, adaptive, entrepreneurial, customer centric, performance driven, innovation driven and so on.

Meanwhile, the inner process of the newly appointed leaders is often quite interesting. Many will see the new order as recognition and appreciation of the talents and style they exhibited in the past, although they've in fact been tasked with shaping a different future with a new way of working.

When leaders start implementing the new strategy, many of them forget to reset their mind. In turbulent times, even when they invest time and energy in working on their mindset, leaders do not sufficiently appreciate that it is in fact about resetting the mind. Under the high pressure that comes with all the changes, human nature holds on to well-known mental and emotional sequences and related behavioural patterns. Old formulas that have brought us success are activated, without even knowing whether these would be viable options for the new situation. In addition, we subconsciously multiply our mistakes without consciously questioning ourselves.

We need a partial mind reset to bring us to the next level. This is a deep personal transformational effort – emotional change is the core catalyst, as our emotions drive our beliefs and this is what drives our behaviour. Transformation is a personal, emotional process. Leadership starts from within. Transforming the team and the bigger organization requires deep personal transformation from the senior leaders first, as role-modelling is the most powerful multiplier. From there we can change the nature of the relationship with others, which is the foundation for building an adaptive culture.

A powerful mind reset starts with self-reflection and requires an intensive dialogue, where the full set of practices, behaviours, beliefs, mindset, values and emotions of the leader are explored and challenged, warmly but firmly. The idea is to find the blind spot or pervasive patterns that limit the transformational leadership power of the leader.

Most leaders have one or two patterns where emotional experiences from the past fix beliefs and drive behaviour that blocks personal progress. Those top-down patterns of behaviour stifle the team and negatively impact the business at large.

Breakthrough conversations help connect the dots, surfacing the ingrained patterns and helping the leader understand why he always makes the same mistakes. Then, ultimately, some deeper emotional exploration helps the leader recognize the related pockets of anger, sadness, guilt or fear that subconsciously feed the dysfunctional patterns.

During these intimate breakthrough conversations, the leader wrestles through a whirl of insights and emotions. This will ideally lead to acknowledgement that the suppressed emotion is actually quite strong, and determines his behaviour under pressure. The pressure amplifies both the readily available and the tightly contained emotions and strengths. The final step involves exploring how a process of genuine forgiveness can help complete the personal transformation. The shadow becomes lighter, immediately expanding the leader's capacity to take on the new role with more depth and finesse.

Understanding the dynamics of 'attachment patterns'[13] is also particularly helpful when exploring the paths for improvement. The quality of attachment bonding with our partners, children and family members determines to a high degree our attachment patterns in business. Research[13] shows that 50% of people have a secure attachment style, while 25% have an anxious attachment style. The remaining 25% have an avoidant attachment style, or a blend of the secure and anxious styles.

This means that in daily practice one out of two adults has an insecure attachment style. These people are on average more responsive than others to triggers generated by shadow behaviours. Consider what it means for a company of 100,000 employees when 50% of its people – 50,000 individuals – have an insecure attachment style. This may provide for a sense of thriving energy in the workplace, but it certainly amplifies dysfunctional behaviour, doomed team interaction and organizational fragmentation, especially under high pressure.

This is an all-too-common reality. As such, it's critically important for senior leaders to be aware of their own, and others' attachment styles in order to provide the team with that all-important sense of safety.

CASE STUDY:
'DO A MIND RESET'

At a large international financial company, almost half of the top 100 executives were asked to move into different roles or leave the company.

Through a carefully planned process, the roles and responsibilities in the top leadership group were re-designed and the senior leaders were nominated into their new positions. This came as a significant part of the bank was preparing to transform itself into an agile new way of working.

During a one-on-one breakthrough coaching conversation, the newly nominated senior leader, who reported directly to the board of directors, shared an interesting observation. He had a deeply held belief that he'd been promoted into his new role because of his loyalty, performance and way of working in the past. He was unaware that he'd actually been promoted to create the new bank and move it into the future. He'd actually been chosen for his potential to shape the future, not to repeat the past.

In his previous roles, he'd fervently believed that he should create the vision, generate the great ideas, crack the difficult issues and then sell his approach to his team so they could implement it. Of utmost importance, he'd always felt, was his need to maintain discipline for implementation. At that time, with a small team of 30 in the broad command and control culture of this global company, that seemed to work.

Now, however, he was facing his first town hall meeting with his new team of 300 people. His major concern was that with only three days to go, he was not clear about what the critical issues were and had no idea what solutions to implement.

He was invited to explore why he thought he needed to always be the smartest kid on the block and why he personally needed to crack the nut. We explored his personal leadership style, at first on the surface and then at a deeper level. To be the best and to be in control were very powerful themes in his stories. Slowly he began to see that in his previous roles he kept problems away from the board and just got things solved. He started to understand that he had been rewarded for his ability to fix problems and maintain tight control. He also started seeing that such an approach just wouldn't work with such a large group of people, and that it certainly wouldn't embody the agile, adaptable approach needed to fundamentally remake a significant piece of the company.

For him to lead the bank's transformation, he would need to change something buried within himself: the root causes, experiences and emotions that activated the repeating pattern of needing to 'be the smartest' and 'be in control'. After some deep, personal reflection the fixed emotions and beliefs dissolved and created the space required for transformation.

He explored using the town hall meeting to invite these 300 people to bring their smartest ideas into the room, and to see himself as the orchestrator. He redefined his role as one of leveraging his brainpower to identify the critical questions he'd ask the group to resolve. By doing so, he would trust his team to start taking ownership and run with it, rather than him driving the implementation and motivating his team. It worked. People can motivate themselves, as long as we invite them to bring their best and stop telling them what to do and how to do it.

He applied the principle of leading from behind, inviting individuals in the group to summon their best talent and energy to find solutions that could be successfully implemented. To achieve the organization's strategic imperatives, he moved from being the smartest kid on the block towards becoming the orchestrator of talent.

Multiply the Inner Compass

7. MULTIPLY THE INNER COMPASS

LEADING FROM PURPOSE AND VALUES

The complexity and intensity of the transformation needed in much of business and society are vast. We cannot do it all by ourselves. In order to bring our best we need one another so that we can multiply our efforts together. And, from a human energy perspective, we need to focus on bringing our best value and attention to those issues and in those time windows that stand to yield the most impact. This requires all players to be energetic and ready for action.

In this era of complexity, uncertainty and seismic shifts in the business and social landscapes, one of the biggest questions for many people is what to hold on to. External references are fading and changing. Therefore, a solid inner compass is necessary to prepare ourselves and our organizations, on every level, for the future.

And, as we've alluded to, one of the biggest constraints these days is shortage of human energy. Demands on people are so high, both at work and in their private lives, that regular 'recharging' is essential for them to be able to continually bring their best. People are frantically busy, more than at any time in human history, yet ineffectiveness causes major energy losses and yields limited impact. The belief that 'less is more' is widely held. Many leaders and their organizations are grappling with how to effectively achieve that ideal.

As noted, everyone has an inner compass that is key to addressing this challenge. The inner compass embodies the golden triangle of purpose, values and vision. When people are invited to jointly explore and share their inner compass, a formidable foundation is established for creating a sense of meaning and belonging. Even better and stronger is the effect of people connecting their own purpose, values and vision to the inner compass of the organization. When their combined inner compasses are brought into synergy, a mighty collective drive can help set the course to a robust future for the organization.

Self-reflection and sharing of our inner compass with others provides a deep source of trust, a shared sense of

meaning and a strong feeling of connectedness. It also fuels passion and maximizes energy levels, generating an endless stream of positive momentum that moves everything forward. Actually, it gives people more energy than it takes from them to achieve common goals. Building a purpose-driven organization, through a leader-driven process that involves people role-modelling across the entire organization, yields a powerful sustained impact.

When we find and live our inner compass we ensure that we'll always be able to bring the best of ourselves and live the life that is our own, not one that is invisibly ruled – and fundamentally hampered – by the expectations of others.

To live our own life, being true to our deepest inner self, requires a granular understanding of our purpose, our true values and our personal vision. Because it matters a lot to us.

One of the biggest revelations for senior leaders is to suddenly gain the insight that they are not living their own true life but are still living reactively to their life script. A helpful question for self-exploration may be: "What hurts you into doing what you do?" Our purpose drives the continuous quest for success, the ultimate acceptance of our true inner self, and seeking to heal our past wounds and trans-generational sufferings – the chronic blues that are transferred from generation to generation.

Purpose gives us drive, values give us guidance when facing dilemmas or difficult choices, and vision gives us an aspirational sense of direction.

When we live in true honesty, consistently following our inner compass, we receive more energy back from life than it takes out of us. It's kind of a perpetual-motion mobile. Life stimulates each of us to find our true path and live it. We can trust others will do the same, so that together we can do what needs to be done.

Co-creating a set of shared values – and living these as role-model leaders throughout the organization – is a critical requirement for a long-lasting trust culture. Value conflicts are among the most painful incidents in relationships. They demolish trust and raise anxiety, not only with the central players, but also across the communities that are directly and indirectly involved or witnessing the incidents. That is why human processes require a careful 'soft touch' approach, meeting people where they are and starting from a place of respect for our differences. This applies not only in the boardroom, which is often home to powerful conflicts and strong shadow fights, but across all levels in the organization.

It's not uncommon to think, "I am separate from you[2] and the two of us are separate from the group." In most cases, nothing could be less true. Instead, think this: "I am in the group and the group is in me." You need to see yourself as a part of the problem, a part of the challenge, in order to become part of the solution.

Time and again, when people get to know each other better, and at a truly deeper level, they're surprised at how much they have in common. It's virtually always more than they initially suspected, once they stop dwelling on what sets them apart through their differences.

Co-creating the vision is a process of synthesis (as opposed to analysis). How can we join our best thoughts together, and build upon each other's ideas? How can we integrate our personal vision into our team and organizational vision? How do we collaborate on building a co-created vision from the inside out? A strong common purpose, strongly lived shared values (including corrective measures for dysfunctional behaviour) and an inspiring co-created vision are essential for trust, speed and adaptive agility. Thus, strategizing becomes an ongoing process.

CASE STUDY:
'MULTIPLY THE INNER COMPASS'

A large retailer was looking for a solution to re-energize its entire staff. Customer centricity and re-vitalizing passion and energy within the business had become critical issues. Restructuring fatigue and a long energy-draining period had raised anxiety levels, significantly reducing employee engagement and sense of ownership across the organization.

When we were asked to step in, we focused on re-centring the top 20 employees, individually and collectively. In a 3.5 day workshop, they were invited to reflect upon their lifelines, share them with each other, and ponder their inner compass (purpose, values, vision).

After having intensively worked on themselves and regaining a normalized level of trust and connectedness, the group was invited to blend their inner compasses into a team compass, projecting it even further into a first sketch of a company-wide compass. As they experienced the power of the transformation process they'd worked through together, they had courageous conversations on what 'great' would look like if they were to convey and multiply this experience across the whole organization.

During the heated debate, they learned how to better manage the shadow dynamics, both from the team's perspective as well as for themselves. They learned to manage emotions in the group, regulate their own breathing to reduce anxiety, control the blame game, empathize with the needs of others in the group, and provide one another with what each person needed to navigate these very emotional conversations. It did not go perfectly – far from it – but it was clearly the beginning of a process of change that played out in a safe, collaborative place. In fact, the team identified solutions to some very pressing issues and expressed a personal commitment to implement them.

Nonetheless, one matter proved stubbornly tough to crack. How can we reach our frontline people in the stores? There was no time to get them out of the store for a one- or two-day transformation workshop. Also, would this approach really shift the needle in a robust way with only one workshop? Consequently, a pilot experiment was created. The idea was to think 'continuous improvement', turning the concept of the two-day workshop into a weekly one-hour session for a total of 13 weeks. The content was redesigned into meaningful hour-long

sessions that were each impactful on their own. During the pilot, the integrative and multiplying power of each step became evident. A weekly 15-minute catch-up conversation helped to sustain the momentum of the main sessions.

Once the concept had proved its effectiveness, a master class for internal HR professionals and store managers was rolled out. Through this simplification of the concept, the 'train the trainer' approach was quite effective.

The core idea of continuous improvement was successful and, after the first cycle of 13 weeks, the wheel kept turning, on and on.

Have Courageous Conversations

8. HAVE COURAGEOUS CONVERSATIONS

SPEAKING YOUR OWN TRUTH

Every single person has an inner compass, where life experiences, beliefs and acquired practices exert their influence on one another, for better or worse. When working with others, we all bring our own strongly ingrained mental models to the table. In any conversations, we bring our past experiences into the room and superimpose them over current considerations. This is often the case with those themes that matter the most to us.

To get the best from everyone, we need to take each individual's mindset, beliefs and emotions as the starting point and work to meet people where they are.[5] Then, trust the good intentions of everyone and believe that every single person can contribute to the solution and help the team move forward.

Invite everyone to speak his or her own truth and you'll be surprised how much people have in common, vis-à-vis the differences that separate them. It is the perfect starting point to build bridges and close gaps between boundaries that the participants perceive. As a leader, learn to speak last and enjoy the wisdom of the team. Invite people to

go through the process and take responsibility and ownership. That will energize and multiply the action power.

Teams need warming up before they can go into high-performance mode. They also require structural and frequent maintenance – in reality, much more than we think they do. As a team leader, first try to focus on what team members have in common; only later explore and integrate the differences, to the extent that that's needed.

Whenever possible, whether in a courageous conversation or during an important decision-making process, apply the 'Mayonnaise Method'. When making mayonnaise, if you want it to be smooth and delicious, and prevent it from separating, drip the oil in slowly. Don't lose patience and pour it all in at once; things just won't come together. A proven process for team decision-making is to focus on a powerful leading question, and then encourage self-reflection within the team. That's followed by asking participants to pair up and talk things through, building on what they have in common, which can be expanded upon as these pairs are gradually merged into larger and larger groups. In this way the entire team – from individuals to small clusters, and onward to the whole group – comes together to explore potential solutions and reach final, collaborative decisions.

Here's a practical set of guiding questions that has proven its power across all hierarchical levels in diverse industry segments:

1. Define and build agreement around what is the key problem we want to resolve.
2. Ask what 'great' would look like in the organization, and what ideas, resources and actions are required to get there.
3. Ask what the potential roadblocks are and what solutions can be proposed.

Change the way all team members talk to one another; this will change the way you look at things and ultimately modify the way you act. If possible, invite people to talk things through as you go for a walk as a team. This is so much more powerful than clicking through PowerPoint charts in a drab, soul-killing conference room.

Think about the number of hours we sit around meeting tables over the course of a week. It's an insidious energy-drain; human beings just aren't built to sit all day. Our nature is to be upright, to be active and to walk. Having more meetings in a 'walk and talk' format is highly recommended.

When we walk and talk, our conversations are less rigidly structured, less informed by anxiety, more open, honest and genuine. The endorphins that are generated as our pulse accelerates, our respiration picks up and the juices get flowing create a more positive mindset. Along the way, when we're energized in this way, we become more adaptive and willing to find common solutions.

Walking is good for our energy levels, and it allows the body to better handle and dissipate tensions that may arise during conversations. In a fluorescent-lit meeting room, this stress would form muscle tension and raise your blood pressure. A tried-and-true conversational technique calls for walking side-by-side and looking in the same direction, rather than sitting opposite each other looking directly at one another's faces.

Researchers at Stanford University found evidence that people's creative thinking increases by as much as 60% when they engage in a walking and talking meeting format.

If, for whatever reason, we cannot walk and talk, and are compelled to meet around a conference table, most people don't realize how much the table itself is blocking our human exchange. In particular, it blocks physical communications (body language) and irrational domains. If you're forced to convene in an office setting, maximum effectiveness can be achieved by sitting in a circle of chairs and talking without a table separating participants. This is the ancient way tribes talked around the campfire.

As we run from meeting to meeting, we have little time to refresh our thinking and regenerate our energy for the next meeting. When we arrive at a meeting, we generally make a cold start, tackling the agenda points one by one. It's common for just one person, or a couple of people, to do most of the talking while the others listen ... or not, depending on whether they think a specific topic may be relevant to them.

We can improve the power of courageous conversations by using the word 'yes' more often.

Without 'yes' nothing can be accomplished. But how do you build a positive culture that actively says 'yes'? How do you get to, "Yes, I like the idea and I'll join you."

In one-on-one conversations we do it rather spontaneously. Once we're in a group, though, anxiety levels spike and we stop actively saying 'yes'. Whenever we say 'yes' the energy of the group starts to shift in a positive direction. Realistically speaking, in conversations we tend to spend most of our time wrestling with the conflicts.

Talk less and consciously say 'yes' more often. Leadership through active followership is a powerful intervention to accelerate business.

CASE STUDY: 'HAVE COURAGEOUS CONVERSATIONS'

A leading global company wanted to reinvent the way it engaged with its top leaders. Six major topics required courageous conversation to unlock the necessary transformation: customer centricity, mindset, execution, entrepreneurship, collaboration and innovation.

The biggest question the CEO grappled with was how to create an inspiring session with so many participants and make significant progress on awareness, ownership and decision-making.

We set out to achieve these multiple goals by paying close attention to designing an effective meeting process. Through co-creation we designed a leadership journey format where 40 groups of six participants each worked on different assignments while walking and talking in nature. Key to this was a set of guiding questions that directed the process. The Q&A construct started at the personal level before talking about the team and the business, constantly wove together individuals' thoughts within the small groups, and then shared these with the gathering at large. Other elements included sharing hot ideas and best practices with colleagues, walks in nature and using handheld tablet devices to enhance the experience, assuring quality control and having a fully self-organized process.

During this exercise, the top leaders engaged in deep conversations about these six critical topics and the urgent transformational change their company required. Conversations were kept focused, highly relevant and of practical value. This helped build trust and generate the best ideas from the collective intelligence of the group, while encouraging ownership at all levels.

After breakfast the small groups were transported to public parks nearby. Each group's leader was in charge of the tablets and knew the day's programme. The groups used the tablets to review the themes. Each session started by setting the scene and with an inspirational video clip, followed by self-reflection and a group discussion. At the end of each session the group's final input on the theme was entered on the tablet and all the data was collected and analysed.

Conclusions were formulated and presented to the entire group on their return to the conference room. Three recommendations were made per theme, plus one outlier/expert recommendation, and these were shared with the larger group. In the next step, participants chose the recommendation that they wanted to work on and reassembled into small groups. After further deliberation, their final results were again entered on the tablets. In the evening, the results were analysed and served as a starting point for the next day's team deliberations, which were geared towards building action plans.

One of the participants provided some very touching feedback. She revealed that she'd never thought it possible to align on such sensitive topics, with such a big group, in such a short timeframe. She said she had never felt such a strong sense of collaboration and alignment in a business setting.

The beauty of the exercise – beyond what would prove to be game-changing team-building, collaboration, recommendations and action plans – was that it didn't even feel like work because of the walks and conversations in nature.

Feedback/
Feedforward

9. FEEDBACK/ FEEDFORWARD

STIMULATING CONTINUOUS IMPROVEMENT

All of us have a deep yearning to be seen, heard and valued. Ultimately, we want to be seen for who we truly are. We all do our utmost, in our own way, to contribute what we think is of value. Sometimes, when we're feeling particularly buoyant, we contribute our light side. Other times, when we're under pressure and experience anxiety, we contribute our shadow side.

Giving honest feedback in a respectful way is the most precious gift we can offer anyone! The simple fact that another person takes the time and pays close attention to 'what I do' and 'who I am' is priceless. It is even better when we get practical feedforward tips on how to improve.

Asking for feedback can be an extremely powerful process, not only for you but also for the people around you. In doing so you role-model new behaviour that others will start to replicate. Asking for feedback is the single most powerful intervention in a people-centric approach.

Feedback is one of the central critical processes in collaboration. The process consists of four major steps: asking, giving, receiving and taking action.

The ultimate objective is to have a feedback culture where everyone across all levels dares to ask for honest feedback. Daring to ask for feedback is the key to building a feedback culture. The role-modelling is the multiplier. Recent studies of large global companies have shown that from the top-down people dare to give honest feedback. It's a different story entirely from a bottom-up perspective, where people fear the repercussions of their honesty.

Receiving feedback is one of the most difficult practices we experience. Due to previous life experiences with

family members, friends, teachers and leaders, we're often fearful of being criticized. So, we tend to shut down before the feedback even arrives in our mind, heart or body. The best approach is to remain open, receive the feedback in its entirety and say thank you. Even if you don't like it – or disagree with the message in that moment – you can still thank the feedback giver for their time and energy. It is ok for you to say you need to think about the feedback, especially if you don't agree with it. Sleep on it, think about it, see what you can learn from it, remain open and receptive. It is only when we let

the feedback touch our feelings that we can build the energy to work on improving.

It is important to remember that the content of any feedback reflects as much about the giver as it does the receiver.

Doing something with the feedback we receive and working on improving is what people around us are waiting for. They expect us to take their feedback seriously and provide evidence of our progress. The most powerful way to work on improving is by creating a performance/learning coalition, where colleagues are integrally involved in the feedback process from beginning to end. They continuously engage with feedback to support a colleague's improvement until the behavioural change becomes embedded.

The lighter, faster and easier approach is feedforward. People learn and dare to ask for tips on how they can improve, and colleagues give them concrete tips when asked. In practice, feedforward is becoming increasingly common since it creates strong forward movement. It brings rigour and no escape for transforming behaviour. Especially when feedforward is applied to mini-habits, the impact of behavioural change is high.

A very special angle to conscious feedback is a focused approach to 'appreciative' feedback. The underlying belief is, "Let's appreciate what is right, so we have the energy to fix what is wrong!"[8]

No matter which methodology you embrace, feedback/feedforward is the most powerful instrument for a business to drive exponential acceleration. It is freely available. The only thing it demands is continuous role-modelling by the top leaders by asking for feedback/feedforward. Apply the Law of Santa Claus. Ask for what you need …

CASE STUDY: 'FEEDBACK/FEEDFORWARD'

A large financial services company had a serious challenge with risk, one of its critical business areas. Leadership decided to pursue a trajectory towards significantly improving team performance. During conversations to prepare for the intervention, it became clear that the group was not cohesive and it was filled with anxieties. Step-by-step, the team was guided through the leading from behind practices. Along the way, participants found common ground and got to know each other on a deeper, more personal level.

This process created a suitable starting point for 'courageous conversations' on relevant business topics. During this dialogue, it became clear that there was a tendency to start conversations about what was not working and to start analysing why. That came with a healthy dose of suggesting who was to blame. The team faced

a barrier as, understandably, emotions increased during these conversations.

Based on common language that was worked out during the initial steps, it became obvious that the team was composed of Fixers, Protectors and, predominantly, Survivors. In the heat of the moment the Protectors started blaming the others, while the Survivors became silent and disappeared under the radar. Talking about what was not going well and exploring the logic behind it drained the team's energy and led participants to begin doubting one another. This all conspired to block the can-do mentality of the group. A major turning point came when the notion of 'feedforward' was introduced and the team learned how it differed from 'feedback'.

We invited the team to start with a different entry point, focusing on feedforward questions and ideas. Where do we want to go? How do we create a path forward? What is the vision? What does it take to get there? How do we get the best from all of us?

By focusing on the vision, the energy in the group went up – the trigger to make it happen was touched. Participants started working on the desired path forward. After that the team asked itself, "What are the learnings from the past that we need to integrate to move forward?" The outcome showed the need to focus on the future in order to move forward. The trust and can-do mentality came back. So did confidence and a genuine belief in the group's ability to make things happen. As the trust and energy returned, the spark was ignited: Onwards!

In conclusion, it is the nature of the question that defines the quality of the answer.

OUR STORY

ENABLING TRANSFORMATIONAL LEADERSHIP

Courage11 is an independent global firm of seasoned practitioners dedicated to the mastery of transformational leadership.

We work with C-level teams of large corporate clients and their senior leaders.

We enable senior executives to get the best leadership from themselves, their teams and their organization. We focus on the power of collective leadership within and across teams to drive growth and value creation. We work from the inside-out and apply stakeholder centred coaching. We systemically strengthen courage throughout organizations and turn it into coordinated traction.

We aim for exponential transformation resulting in 1+1 = 11. Courage11.

Our work is grounded in cutting edge, simple, robust and easy-to-learn practices that work across all cultures and organizational levels. Our way of working is humble, intense, truthful and actionable. The intensity of our work has a deep and lasting impact on the people and the business.

We guide, role-model and build capabilities for transformational leadership. We coach, train and facilitate senior leaders, their teams and organizations to achieve high

impact business, leadership and cultural transformation. We continuously develop innovative ways and digital solutions to make the transformation stick.

We live our values in action:
Love – Always assume good intent.
Courage – To experience the anxiety and still do what you have to do.
Action – To build a better world.
Pragmatism – What works is what's right.
Making a difference – A better life for everyone we touch.

ABOUT THE
AUTHORS

DIRK DEVOS

Dirk is an international expert in leading high impact change with a particular emphasis on large system interventions, leadership development, family systems theory and organizational learning. Dirk works with clients in a range of different industries, including Financial Services, FMCG, Professional Service Firms, Retail, Energy, Process Industry and Education.

His interventions are minimalistic and strive to evolve ownership and responsibility from the first moment onwards. He is strong in helping senior leaders build trust among one another and throughout the organization, while at the same time building a high-performing climate of challenge and drive for execution.

Dirk guides senior leaders and their teams to achieve robust strategic impact. His expertise includes personal and team guidance, an integrated approach of strategy and leadership development, high impact execution power, intercultural cooperation and strategic breakthrough innovation.

He focuses on helping leaders shift the core of the organizational DNA towards sustainable high performance.

Previously Dirk was a partner at several global leadership boutique firms. He is a graduate of the MIT/Dialogos Strategic Dialogue Master's programme. He is co-author of *21 Leaders for the 21st Century*, elaborating on core values and win-win dilemma strategies in an intercultural business context.

Over time he has developed deeply rooted, integrated and validated practice capabilities in many different roles, including boardroom advisor, executive coach, strategy consultant, organizational development consultant, change process and workshop designer and facilitator, team coach, trainer, train-the-trainer lead, consultant's consultant, guide for high impact learning journeys, dialogue facilitator and trusted guide for personal development work.

Dirk is fluent in Dutch, English, French and German.

MANON DE WIT

Manon de Wit is an international expert in leading high impact change, coaching and communication, focused on increasing collective leadership and business performance of individuals, teams and organizations.

She has a passion for enabling leaders to develop their unique and most impactful leadership style. She is particularly skilled at coaching and facilitating diverse groups and individuals. She coaches C-level executives and senior leaders with major global companies. Her goal is to get the best out of individuals and teams to create breakthroughs in business performance. Her deep belief is that courageous conversations, feedback/ feedforward and co-creation will lead to the best result. Dialogic skills are crucial in this process and this has her special attention.

Manon believes that there is significant untapped potential in each individual and in every team. She starts by taking a deep dive into patterns of behaviour. Her coaching is to the point, insightful, inspiring and energizing, based on the systemic human needs: bonding, order and balance. Manon's coaching is all about accelerating and deepening personal growth, beyond what people have thought possible. The outcome is an enriched set of functional patterns of behaviour, while Manon also helps individuals and teams get rid of their dysfunctional patterns and increase personal resilience. In order to get there, she creates awareness of defence mechanisms and personal masks.

With her down-to-earth pragmatism and her inclination to see the sunny side of things, people experience Manon as a warm, efficient and skillful coach who enables one to get out of their comfort zone in a safe way. She opens up people who never opened up before and creates personal and professional breakthroughs.

Previously, Manon was a partner at a global leadership firm. She is an expert in team dynamics, organization system theory and experience-based learning.

Manon works in Dutch and English and understands German.

ROBERT LUBBERDING

Robert is an international expert in leading business transformation. His expertise includes executive coaching, teambuilding, culture change, leadership development, talent management, change management, organizational governance, programme management and strategy execution. Robert was previously a partner at several professional services firms, where he was responsible for the People and Change practice, locally and internationally.

Robert guides senior leaders and their teams in creating high strategic impact. He combines strategy and leadership development in change approaches that align and engage people in the organization, and focuses on building a leadership capability that fosters a culture of high performance and getting things done. In his consulting work, Robert also draws on his personal and practical experience of leading his own practices and being a member of the management board in various consulting firms through upturns and downturns over more than two decades.

He worked on major change programmes for a wide variety of companies in Europe and America, in industries including Education, Engineering, Financial Services, FMCG, Manufacturing, Professional Service Firms, Process Industry and Retail.

Over time he has worked in a number of different roles as boardroom advisor, executive coach, strategy consultant, change architect, facilitator (including on large-scale programmes), trainer, train-the-trainer lead and program manager.

Robert works in Dutch, English and German.

REFERENCES/ BIBLIOGRAPHY

REFERENCES

1. Lane, David; Maxfield, Robert. *"Strategy under complexity: Fostering generative relationships."* Long Range Planning (1996): 215-231.

2. Agazarian, Yvonne. *System-Centered Therapy For Groups.* New York: The Guildford Press, 1997.

3. Hellinger, Bert. *Family Constellations Revealed: Hellinger's Family and other Constellations Revealed: Volume 1 (The Systemic View).* Antwerp: Indra Torsten Preiss, 2012.

4. Kantor, David. *Reading the Room.* San Francisco: Jossey-Bass, 2012.

5. Isaacs, Williams. *Dialogue and the Art of Thinking Together.* New York: Doubleday, 1999.

6. Cooperrider, David; Kaplin Whitney, Daina. *Appreciative Inquiry.* San Francisco: Berrett Koehler Communications, 1999.

7. Bourbeau, Lise. *Heal Your Wounds & Find Your True Self.* Saint-Jerome, Quebec: Les Editions ET.C. Inc., 2001.

8. *Celebrate what's right - the film.* Last modified 2018. http://celebratewhatsright.com/film-0

9. Scharmer, Otto. *Theory U: Leading from the Future as It Emerges.* San Francisco: Berret-Koehler Publishers, Inc., 2009.

10. Senge, Peter; Scharmer, Otto; Jaworski, Joseph; Flowers, Berry Sue. *Presence: An Exploration of Profound Change in People, Organizations, and Society.* New York: Crown Business, 2008.

11. Lutkehaus, Nancy. *Margaret Mead: The Making of an American Icon.* Princeton NJ: Princeton University Press, 2008, p. 261.

12. Goldsmith, Marshall; Reiter, Mark. *What Got You Here Won't Get You There: How Successful People Become Even More Successful.* New York: Hyperion, 2007.

13. Levine, Amir; Heller, Rachel. *Attached: The New Science of Adult Attachment and How it Can Help You Find - and Keep – Love.* New York: Penguin Group, 2010.

BIBLIOGRAPHY

This book is highly influenced by the work of:

Agazarian, Yvonne. *System-Centered Therapy For Groups*. New York: The Guildford Press, 1997.

Berne, Eric. *Games people play: The Basic Handbook of Transactional Analysis*. New York: Ballantine Books, 1964.

Bohm, David. *On Dialogue*. London and New York: Routledge, 1996.

Bourbeau, Lise. *Heal Your Wounds & Find Your True Self*. Saint-Jerome, Quebec: Les Editions ET.C. Inc., 2001.

Celebrate what's right - the film. Last modified 2018. http://celebratewhatsright.com/film-0

Cooperrider, David; Kaplin Whitney, Daina. *Appreciative Inquiry*. San Francisco: Berrett Koehler Communications, 1999.

Drucker, Peter. *Managing in Turbulent Times*. New York: Routledge, 2011.

Gawdat, Mo. Solve for Happy: Engineer Your Path to Joy. New York: Simon & Schuster, Inc., 2017.

Goldsmith, Marshall; Reiter, Mark. *What Got You Here Won't Get You There: How Successful People Become Even More Successful*. New York: Hyperion, 2007.

Goldsmith, Marshall; Reiter, Mark. *Triggers: Sparking positive change and making it last*. London: Profile Books LTD, 2015.

Harari, Yuval N. *Sapiens: A Brief History of Humankind*. First U.S. edition. New York, NY: Harper, 2015.

Harari, Yuval N. *Homo Deus: A Brief History of Tomorrow*. First U.S. edition. New York: Harper, an imprint of HarperCollins Publishers, 2017.

Hellinger, Bert. *Family Constellations Revealed: Hellinger's Family and other Constellations Revealed: Volume 1 (The Systemic View)*. Antwerp: Indra Torsten Preiss, 2012.

Hill, Laura. *"Leading from Behind." Harvard Business Review*. May 5, 2010. Accessed December 1, 2017. https://hbr.org/2010/05/leading-from-behind.

Isaacs, Williams. *Dialogue and the Art of Thinking Together*. New York: Doubleday, 1999.

Ismail, Salim; Malone, Michael; Van Geest, Yuri; Diamandis, Peter. *Exponential Organizations: Why new organizations are ten times better, faster, and cheaper than yours (and what to do about it)*. New York: Diversion Books 2014.

Kantor, David. *Reading the Room*. San Francisco: Jossey-Bass, 2012.

Lane, David; Maxfield, Robert. *"Strategy under complexity: Fostering generative relationships."* *Long Range Planning* (1996): 215-231.

Levine, Amir; Heller, Rachel. *Attached: The New Science of Adult Attachment and How it Can Help You Find - and Keep – Love*. New York: Penguin Group 2010.

Lutkehaus, Nancy. *Margaret Mead: The Making of an American Icon*. Princeton NJ: Princeton University Press, 2008, p. 261.

Mandela, Nelson. *Long Walk to Freedom: the autobiography of Nelson Mandela*. London: Abacus, 2003.

Patterson, Kerry; Grenny, Joseph; McMillan, Ron; Switzler, Al. *Crucial Conversations: Tools for Talking when Stakes are High*. USA: McGraw-Hill, 2012.

Raworth, Kate. *Doughnut Economics: 7 Ways to Think Like a 21ˢᵗ Century Economist*. Vermont: Chelsea Green Publishing, 2017.

Scharmer, Otto. *Theory U: Leading from the Future as It Emerges*. San Francisco: Berret-Koehler Publishers, Inc., 2009.

Senge, Peter M. *The Fifth Discipline: the Art and Practice of the Learning Organization*. New York: Doubleday/Currency, 1990.

Senge, Peter; Scharmer, Otto; Jaworski, Joseph; Flowers, Berry Sue. *Presence: An Exploration of Profound Change in People, Organizations, and Society*. New York: Crown Business, 2008.

Sinek, Simon. *Start With Why: How Great Leaders Inspire Everyone to Take Action*. New York: Portfolio / Penguin, 2011.

Weick, Karl; Roberts, Karlene. *"Collective Mind in Organizations: Heedful Interrelating on Flight Decks."* *Administrative Science Quarterly* (1993): 357-381.

Attention is the rarest and purest
form of generosity.

Simone Weil

Never doubt that a small group
of thoughtful, committed people
can change the world. Indeed,
it is the only thing that ever has.

Margaret Mead

Courtesy
All pictures in this book have been taken by the participants of our journeys and the Courage11 team.
We are grateful to have experienced the stunning beauty of nature all around the world.